ISBN-13: 978-1545140611
ISBN-10: 1545140618
Printed in the United States of America

L.I.F.E. Publishing Co.
PO Box 17412
Winston-Salem, NC 27116

40 Days of Surrender
Journey to the Heart of God

KAREN MARSHALL JENNINGS

DEDICATION

To Mom,
my Best Friend
Thank you for always
believing in me!!

and

To Dad,
Thank you for always
encouraging me!!

BOOKS IN THIS SERIES

40 Days of Surrender: Journey to the Heart of God

40 Days of Surrender: Journey to the Heart of God
Large Print Version

40 Days of Surrender: Journey to the Heart of God
eBook Version

40 Days of Surrender Journal for Women

40 Days of Surrender Journal for Men

CONTENTS

CHAPTER 1
THE RICH YOUNG RULER AND I

"No, Father," I pleaded. "Please don't ask me to give that up!"

I had been willing to give up everything to follow Jesus; just not that. How could I live without it?

I had drifted away from the closeness my Father and I shared. I wasn't sure why. But, I wanted to have that intimate relationship with Him once more.

For several days I had been asking God to open my eyes and show me anything that was coming between us. I thought I was willing to give up anything to have that familiar relationship back.

God had begun to show me many things. I had allowed items to come into my home and my life that weren't pleasing to Him. They were hurting our relationship. As a result, I had filled many garbage bags full of items and taken them to the dump. This was the beginning of a

1

closer walk with Him. I could tell that our communication was getting back on track. I was excited to continue the process.

However, this particular day, God asked me to give up something that was very precious to me; something I thought I couldn't live without. Had I heard wrong?

God didn't speak to me in an audible voice. It wasn't always clear to me what He was saying. When I was younger, I often misinterpreted His messages, usually to justify something I wanted. But, over the years, I had learned to distinguish His voice from my own by making sure it aligned with Scripture. I also made sure it wasn't something that would benefit only me.

It's difficult to describe how God spoke to me that day. I felt His response in my heart and my mind when I prayed. It was that still, small voice, so quiet that it could be drowned out by distractions or other thoughts… unless I listened very closely. When I did, it was as though He was actually speaking to me.

I knew God spoke to me through His Word. I decided to double check with the Bible. I opened it and sought the wisdom that I knew its pages held. This is my summary of the story I read that day in Luke 18:18-23.

> There was a rich, young ruler who wanted to follow Jesus. He came and asked Him, "Good Teacher, what shall I do to inherit eternal life?"

Jesus knew the man's heart well. There were three things he needed help with. Jesus subtly pointed these out to the young man.

Jesus first addressed the man's insincere praise. He was trying to flatter Jesus by calling Him good. I imagine that, being a rich ruler, he learned the art of flattery in order to further his own interests. Jesus wasn't having any of that. I like to think that He was essentially saying, "Why are you trying to butter me up? That won't work on Me."

The second issue was his lack of repentance. Although the man didn't say much, Jesus knew what was in his heart. In order to accept Jesus as your Savior you have to know that you are not perfect. We are all sinners saved by God's grace. When Jesus told him he needed to keep the commandments, he claimed that he had never sinned. He had no need to repent.

The third problem was his money. Jesus knew that it was his security. He depended on his riches instead of trusting in God. When Jesus asked him to sell it all and give the proceeds to the poor, he said in his heart, "No way!" Then he walked away sad.

I realized that I had been doing the same thing. Jesus had asked me to give up something that I wasn't ready to surrender. Was I going to be like the rich, young ruler? Was I going to walk away sad?

CHAPTER 2
RECEIVING MY CALLING

Many years earlier...

I met Jesus and accepted Him as my Savior when I was 16 years old. My life changed dramatically. I went from being a rebellious teen to a loving daughter. I felt very close to my heavenly Father. We had an intense relationship.

Hungering to know Him more intimately, I devoured the Scriptures for many hours each day. I couldn't get enough of His Word. I wanted to know Him better and reading His love letters to me was the best way I knew to accomplish that. I listened to Christian music as well, praising Him continually in everything that I did. It was a beautiful relationship!

I longed to serve Him. I was overflowing with joy and sought His will for my life. I volunteered at church. I witnessed to my unsaved friends. I did what I could, although I didn't really know where I belonged within the family of God or what my divine purpose was.

After high school, I began taking classes at a local community college. I was especially drawn to the writing courses. The teacher was amazing! He was very encouraging and I excelled under his training. This encouragement seemed to awaken a primal need within me: a need to write. I began crafting stories in my spare time. I even kept a notebook next to my bed in case I woke up with an idea that I wanted to remember.

My first semester of college was when I began to get excited about writing. But, it was in my second year that I received my calling.

Walking around campus, I began seeing signs for a Christian Writer's Conference. I had no idea what it was all about but, for some strange reason, it thrilled me! I knew I had to be a part of it. I signed up that very day to attend all of the workshops. I felt that something amazing was going to happen there. I couldn't wait for the day to come!

Several weeks later, that day finally arrived. There was a flurry of people all buzzing about. I came prepared, carrying a big pad of paper and several writing instruments. I didn't want to miss one single word of what they had to teach me about the profession of writing. I was hungry to know everything!

There were all sorts of workshops. Some concentrated on preparing your manuscripts for publication. Others were on actual writing techniques, deciphering writer's jargon, or how to handle rejection. There were so many things this novice writer needed to know. My mind was whirling. I felt as though I had been thrown into a pool and was learning to swim. Yet, it thrilled me. It opened up a whole new world of possibilities.

I had attended several of the workshops, taking notes as fast as I could. In the minutes between classes, I would ask the speaker to explain anything I had missed or didn't understand. There was so much to learn. I was soaking it all in and having the time of my life.

Then, I walked into my next class. It was entitled, Writing For God. I had no idea what that would entail, but I knew I was right where I was supposed to be. I could feel it. I had my pen in hand and paper in front of me. I was ready to take notes. However, when I heard the speaker refer to writing as a calling from God, I set my pen down and looked up. I became captivated as he told his story of how God called him to write. He talked of his struggles and his victories. Then he spoke of how he was using his writing to glorify God. I listened intently as the Holy Spirit stirred within my heart. I knew that was exactly what I wanted to do. By the end of the conference, I was certain that my Father was calling me to write for Him.

I met several ladies at the conference who invited me to join their critique group. It was a wonderful bunch of diverse women, who had two things in common. They were all Christians and they loved to write!

We gathered once a week to read our latest composition and to encourage one another. The group shared ideas on ways to improve our drafts. When anyone had a manuscript published, we rejoiced together. It felt very reassuring to have fellow Christians with whom I could discuss my writing.

I practiced the art of polishing a manuscript and submitting it for publication. The rejection letters didn't bother me much. I had been taught that a writer was not successful until they'd received 2,000 rejections. With each one, I learned something new. I continued to gain experience.

Soon I began to see some success. I wrote a lot of short stories and poems. Many were eventually published, mostly in Sunday School papers and church magazines. I also wrote special interest pieces for a newspaper. My calling was becoming a reality.

CHAPTER 3
BEGINNING A CAREER

God's calling for me was clear. My purpose in life was to encourage others through my writing. I continued to pursue a degree in English, with that motive in mind.

Every spare moment I was writing short stories that glorified God. All of my college writing assignments displayed my love for the Father. Christian professors encouraged this aspect of my writing. Non-believing teachers, on the other hand, were less than thrilled with it and discouraged writing on "religious" subjects. I was so in love with my Lord that I just couldn't help but reflect it in all of my writing.

Learning more with every writing course I took, I focused on taking every class the college offered on English, writing, literature, or poetry. I enjoyed learning about these subjects so much that I hadn't stopped to make a plan. I hadn't thought about what type of degree I would complete or what I would do after college.

It wasn't until a couple of years into my education, that I finally sat down with my advisors. We discussed my degree and possible career opportunities. Until then, I just naturally assumed that I would be a writer. I hadn't thought about what that meant or how I would earn a living. My advisors encouraged writing as a helpful skill, but they could not give me any promising prospects for careers in that field. They suggested journalism or teaching English, but I knew neither of those careers was for me.

After that meeting, I started to be concerned with how I would make a living. I knew God had called me to be a writer. I had even had many stories and poems published. As thrilling as it was to see my works in print, I hadn't made much money. I would have to sell about 200 articles a week just to pay my expenses. At that point, I was selling about one in every twenty stories that I wrote. That meant I would have to write four thousand stories a week. How could I possibly do that?

Doubts began to fill my mind. Did God intend me to write as a career or just a hobby? I began to question everything that, until then, I had taken on faith. Eventually, I took the focus off my calling from God and started listening to the counselors. They were pushing me to make a decision soon. Finally, I came to the conclusion that I needed to seek a profession where I could realistically earn a living.

———————

Psychology was another field that had captured my interest. I loved understanding what made people act the way they did. Learning about relationship dynamics and communication was fascinating to me. I didn't think I could earn a living at writing, so I concentrated further education on psychology.

I continued to write stories, however, and I took all of the English courses that I could fit into my schedule. I wasn't ready to give up totally on writing. I told myself I could do both.

While still in college, I completed an internship at a workshop for people with special needs. I developed a deep respect and love for these individuals. Their positive attitudes amazed me. They listened attentively and did their work without complaining. When meeting someone new, they accepted them right away. They never judged or looked down on anyone. I felt right at home there.

Through the years, I held a variety of positions in the field of social work. From family homes to group homes, from churches, schools, and hospitals to parks and gyms, I had the opportunity to counsel in a wide variety of settings. I became an expert in dealing with all sorts of disabilities including mental retardation and developmental disabilities, cerebral palsy, autism, traumatic brain injury, even alcoholism, and substance abuse. Age groups ranged from five to eighty-five. There was diversity in culture, religion, and ethnic groups. Everyone I worked with was unique.

I grew to love counseling. I loved the people I worked with. The more experience I obtained in that field, the more my career grew in that direction. Writing began to take a back seat to social work.

CHAPTER 4
DISTRACTED BY LIFE

Life has a way of changing things. Before I knew it, I had been married and divorced. I found myself a single mother of four beautiful children. I worked as a counselor but still hadn't completed my education. My life was full. I had hopes of fulfilling my calling to write. But, that would have to wait.

Struggling to make ends meet, I couldn't afford a four-year school right away. I wanted to complete my college degree. However, with my busy schedule, I could only take one or two classes per semester. I slowly progressed through community college, taking all of the transferable classes that I could manage.

Ten long years later, I finally graduated with my Associate's Degree in Psychology. I only lacked one more English class to obtain a second Associate's Degree in English.

Having enough credits to count for three years of junior college, I decided it was time to move on.
By then, my children ranged in age from 6 to 14 years old.

I applied and was accepted to a four-year college. Thanks to the extra classes, I was considered a junior. Due to my busy family and work schedule, I continued to take the minimum amount of classes.

———————

Several years later, I was given an opportunity for better employment. It was the break I had been looking for. But, it would mean moving 700 miles away. After much discussion and deliberation, I decided that moving would be in the best interest of us all. It also meant leaving college with only three more classes to graduation.

The new job worked out well and we adjusted to our new environment. I didn't think about college or writing for several years. When my two youngest children became seniors in high school, however, I grew motivated. I made it a goal to graduate at the same time they did.

I contacted the advisor from my school. She put me in touch with one of my teachers, who agreed to supervise my work long distance. (This was before long distance learning became so prevalent.) I made arrangements to take my last two semesters and signed up for classes. It felt good to be working on my goals again. I was reviving my dream.

The following year, there were three graduates in our family. It was a happy time. New and exciting opportunities became available to us. My two oldest children made the decision to move back to our hometown. The two youngest pursued their dream of going to college. I had fulfilled my goal of receiving my Bachelor's Degree with a major in Counseling and a minor in Writing. I had fulfilled my educational goal. I had finally graduated! I could check that off my list.

With all of the children gone, the house was very quiet. I missed them terribly. But, they were pursuing their dreams and I was happy for them. Only now, I had nothing to work on. I had no children to look after. I had no courses to study. There was a void in my life that screamed to be filled. I wanted to be useful again. But how?

What about writing? I had spent many years scribbling down all of the ideas that flowed into my head. I had published some short stories and articles. Other than that, I didn't have much to show for it except boxes crammed full of ideas. There was even a novel that I started but hadn't had time to complete. It was a long time since I had written with a purpose. By then, I thought that the excitement and passion had burned out. But, there was still a spark.

There was, of course, my work. Over the years, I had become very good at what I did. I enjoyed it. Plus, I could earn a good living doing that. My supervisor had been asking me to take on more clients. That meant working over-time, which meant helping more people as well as filling the void that had been left in my life. I didn't take time to pray about it. I simply agreed.

CHAPTER 5
YEARNING FOR MORE

I began working long hours; about 70 a week. I was helping special needs children and their families. We became very close. It filled the void in my empty nest. I couldn't imagine not seeing them every day.

When I came home in the evenings, I was usually exhausted. I'd fix a quick supper and sit down to write. However, most of the time, I found that my mind was as blank as the page in front of me. I kept trying to keep the dream of writing for God alive. But, deep in my heart, I wondered if it would ever become a reality.

I had been a Christian for almost 32 years. I read the Bible, prayed, and had devotions every morning. I went to church every Sunday and had good, Christian friends. Yet I felt that there was something hindering my relationship with God. I didn't know what it was. I just knew, deep in my heart, there was something coming between God and me. I wanted to restore our relationship. But I didn't know where to start.

Easter was fast approaching. I became interested in reading about Christ's resurrection. He spent 40 days on earth before He ascended into heaven. During that time, He appeared to over 500 witnesses. He encouraged His followers to continue in the faith.

After His ascension, those scared people, hiding behind locked doors, became empowered and bold. Their transformations were incredible! They flung open the doors and embarked on a mission to spread the gospel of Jesus wherever they went. These men and women accomplished amazing things for the kingdom of God... all because Christ encouraged them for 40 days.

I wanted to be like them. I wanted to be encouraged by Christ. I wanted to be transformed and fulfill my calling courageously and confidently! But, how was I going to accomplish that?

I began to look more closely at Jesus' life. Before He began His ministry, the Holy Spirit guided him into the wilderness for 40 days. There, he fasted and prayed and was tempted by the devil. He never gave in. He defeated satan with the Word of God. But, He was not quoting from the book. The Word was hidden in his heart. He came forth
triumphant.

There seemed to be something special about 40 days. It seemed that every time I picked up my Bible I would find a reference to 40 days. I decided to make a list. Every time that I read about 40 days or 40 years, I would add it to my list. Soon, I had more than 20 entries. My list included Jesus, His disciples, Noah, Joshua, Jonah and the people of Nineveh, David and Goliath, and Moses. All of these people went through crucial periods of 40 days or 40 years.

Jesus started and ended His ministry with periods of 40 days.

Jesus' disciples began their ministries by spending 40 incredible days with Jesus after His resurrection.

God prepared and preserved Noah and his family before He made it rain for 40 days and 40 nights. They were the only ones on the earth to survive. God used them to repopulate the earth.

Joshua spied out the Promised Land for 40 days. Later, he went on to lead the Hebrews into this land, which became Israel.

Jonah was sent to warn the sinful people in Nineveh of God's impending judgment. He delivered the message that in 40 days God would destroy them. However, when they repented for 40 days in sackcloth and ashes, God had mercy on them and did not destroy them.

Goliath taunted the Israelites for 40 days before David ended his life. That was also the beginning of David's preparation to become king.

I left Moses until last because his life was filled with 40-day and 40-year time frames.

His life itself was a series of 40 year periods. From age 0 to 40, Moses was miraculously saved from death and raised in the palace by the daughter of Pharaoh. For 40 years, he was the Prince of Egypt.

At age 40, he killed an Egyptian to protect a Hebrew slave (one of his people). When it was discovered, he had to flee. So, from age 40 to 80, he made a new life for himself in the wilderness.

At age 80, God called Moses from the burning bush. He told him to return to Egypt and deliver His people from bondage. (If you want to read more about it, the story can be found in Exodus.)

From age 80 until his death, you guessed it, 40 years later, he delivered his people from Egypt and was their leader. During that time, he spent at least two 40-day periods up on Mt. Sinai with God. Very significant things happened during those 40 days.

The first time, God wrote the Ten Commandments on tablets of stone. When Moses returned, triumphantly carrying this Word from God, he found his people caught up in abominable sin. He became so angry and discouraged that he broke the tablets.

The second time he went up on the mountain, God rewrote the Ten Commandments. He also allowed Moses to look upon His back as He went by. Moses was changed so much by his encounters with God that his face glowed for many days afterward. He wore a veil to protect the people's eyes when they looked upon him.

All of these Biblical examples demonstrated to me that 40 days is significant. As I pondered this list, I realized that wherever 40 days or 40 years was mentioned, some momentous event had taken place. This was powerful!

Could God really transform me in 40 days? I hoped He would. I wanted our intimate relationship back. I wanted to feel close to Him once more. I wanted my life to be significant. That is when I decided I would spend 40 days getting back in touch with God.

CHAPTER 6
MY 40-DAY JOURNEY BEGINS

I began on Easter, the same day that Christ had begun encouraging His disciples before His ascension into heaven. I marked the 40 days on a calendar. I also kept a journal. I wanted to record everything that God spoke to me.

I got down on my knees with my open Bible in front of me. Closing my eyes to the distractions around me, I humbly bowed my head. My first prayer was a simple one.

"Lord, open-my eyes. Show me anything that might be coming between us. I love You and I don't want anything to hinder our relationship."

Then I quietly listened for God's still, small voice. Thoughts began to swirl in my mind. Some were just mine; like people I had to see that day or places I had to go. I had to empty my mind of the busy-ness of my life.

I prayed again and listened quietly. Thoughts began coming to my mind. I recalled some items in my home that gave me guilty feelings whenever I saw them. They were things that didn't honor God. I listened a little longer, but I just kept being reminded of those items.

I believed God was showing me this, so I got up and immediately proceeded to get rid of anything in my home that would be dishonoring to my Lord. Our relationship was much more important to me than any material possession.

The first thing I thought of was my movie collection. Although they were all rated PG or PG-13, I knew some of the content didn't honor God. Watching people being portrayed as heroes while they were engaged in sinful behavior was not the way to God's heart. Why did I keep those things that I knew did not please Him?

I remembered the story of the frog who, when placed in a pot of cold water, would not hop out even as the temperature grew hotter. He stayed there until he boiled to death.

I was like that. I had become desensitized to the things of the world... except, for me, it wasn't too late.

It was as though God took off my blinders. I could see clearly that these items were harmful to my soul and that I shouldn't have them in my home.

I had been taught not to be wasteful. So, my first thought was to give these things away instead of trashing them.

However, God impressed on me that they would be just as harmful to others as they were to me. Understanding that, I had no problem getting rid of them.

I was already feeling better. I wrote of the experience in my journal. I wanted to be able to look back and read about this amazing day that was bringing me closer to my heavenly Father.

I threw away garbage bags full of movies that day. I carried out the trash on my way to work.

Day two arrived. I looked forward to meeting with God today. Yesterday's experience had shown me that God was ready and willing to help me get back into fellowship with Him.

I tried to pray but distractions kept creeping in. I could not concentrate on God at all. My mind was flooded by things I had to do that day or people I had to see. Even little noises outside my window captured my attention. I tried reading Scripture but that didn't quiet my thoughts.

Then, I put on some Christian music. It was softly playing in the background while I prayed. Then one song in particular came on. It was a prayer of surrender. I found myself praying the lyrics. It helped to keep my mind focused on my prayer. I was able to concentrate and surrender to God.

As I prayed, God brought to mind other things I had in the house that didn't please Him. I thought I had gotten it all out yesterday. I continued to pray until that seemed to be all I was thinking about. I thanked God for making me aware of more things I could do that would improve our relationship.

Then, I got up and searched the house, looking at it from God's perspective. I could hardly believe the things I found! Things of this world had crept into my house without me even recognizing them. Why hadn't I seen them before?

I took more garbage bags out with me as I left for work.

———————

On day three, I was very excited to see what God had in store for me next.

It turned out to be more of the same. Father showed me other things in my home that were coming in-between Him and me. Gone. No problem. I didn't want anything to interfere with our relationship. It felt good to be rid of items that had made me feel guilty all these years. I was feeling closer and closer to God.

Again, I carried out bags of garbage before I headed off to work.

CHAPTER 7
WRESTLING WITH GOD

Day four arrived. I was ready for more purging. I felt so close to God; more so than I had in a long time. I wanted to get even closer.

Bowing my head, I prayed, "Lord, show me anything that is coming between us. Your love for me is limitless! I know that You want the very best for me. So, I surrender to Your will."

I became quiet then. Taking a deep breath, I slowly loosened the grip that I had on my life. Emotionally, I let go of my goals and dreams. Opening my arms and my heart to whatever God had planned for me, I surrendered. I wanted only His will for my life.

I waited. I listened for God to speak. Expectantly, I wanted Him to open my eyes to more material possessions that I could easily throw away. However, on this day, He presented a very different message.

A feeling came over me that, as He did with Abraham, God was going to ask me to give up my Isaac. Somehow I knew that He would ask me to give up something very precious to me.

The thought then flooded into my mind, "I want you to quit your job."

"Wait! What!?!" I questioned. "Quit my job?" Where did that come from?

I thought I had heard wrong. I grew silent, refocused, and listened again. But, soon the same thought rushed through my mind. "I want you to quit your job."

I couldn't shake it. Obviously, it was a mistake. "God, surely You don't want me to quit my job," I questioned out loud.

By then, I was on my feet, pacing the room. "My job is not only my income, God, but my clients are like family! They depend on me."

"No! I can't do it, God," I adamantly refused.

I left for work feeling perplexed and uneasy.

———

The fifth morning arrived. I prayed as I had before, "Lord, speak to me. Show me what is coming between us. I want to purge it all. I want to be ever so close to you, Father. Open my eyes."

I was hoping to hear about more items I could throw in the trash that would bring me closer to Him. But instead, I heard again, "I want you to quit your job."

Why were these thoughts plaguing me? Was this message really from God? It certainly wasn't my idea. I loved my job! Why would God ask me to do such a thing? It didn't make any sense to me.

I tried to push the thought away. Yet, I wanted God to speak to me. I wanted to know what His will was for my life.

I refocused my mind on God. "Be still, and know that I am God," I quoted from Psalm 46:10.

I tried to empty my mind of any distractions. "Father, show me Your will."

My mind drifted to my true calling. I knew that God had called me to write for Him. He had been patient with me during the years I was raising my children. Then, I thought about how my writing had suffered since I'd started working so many hours. I would come home too exhausted to do anything.

Then I heard it once more, "I want you to quit your job."

Sadness fell over me at the thought of giving up not only my source of income, but the clients and families that had become so precious to me.

I pushed the thought from my mind once again. "I'm sorry, God, but I just can't do it," I wailed as I walked out the door.

I was sad and troubled all day long. Each client that I met with looked to me for physical and emotional support. We had a special bond. They needed me.

I loved them and I needed them to need me. Picturing myself not working with them was heartbreaking.

Day six came. I put on Christian music, hoping that, somehow, it would change the message God put on my heart that day.

I quieted myself and listened for God's still, small voice. I was a little apprehensive about what I would hear.

God hadn't changed His mind. The message came clearly. "I want you to quit your job."

"Ahhh!" I cried out in frustration, "Why are You doing this to me, God?"

Still refusing to listen to Him, I stormily went off to work.

I struggled with the concept throughout the day. What would I do for money if I quit my job? How would I support myself? What about the families I worked with?

How would they get along without me? More personally, how would I get along without them? I just couldn't do it.

CHAPTER 8
ACCEPTANCE AND GOD'S POWER

The sun rose on day seven. I was tired. I didn't want to hear the same message from my Father. I had grown weary of arguing with God. But, I wanted desperately to have a closer relationship with Him. So, in repentance, I sunk to my knees.

"All right, God," I cried. "I surrender. I am willing to do whatever you ask. If it is Your will that I quit my job, I will do it. I know you will always be with me. I trust You, Lord." I lifted my hands high in surrender. "Lord Jesus, I give You complete control."

Suddenly, a great peace flowed over my soul. In my heart, I felt God was saying to me, "I am with you. Don't be afraid."

I awaited more instructions. But, to my complete surprise, I didn't hear anything more. Was this just a test like when God asked Abraham to sacrifice Isaac? Did He only want me to be willing to surrender? I could only guess. God was quiet after that. With an overwhelming peace in my heart, I climbed into my car and drove to work.

I went to see my first client. We worked on the usual goals. Nothing seemed different. But I was filled with peace and an overwhelming joy. I felt closer to God than I had in a very long time. During my time there, I received a phone call from my supervisor. It was nothing unusual. She simply asked if I would stop by the office when I was done with my client. I probably forgot to sign some paperwork.

As I pulled my car into the office parking lot, I felt God's Spirit and strength working in me. I entered the building and several of my coworkers greeted me cheerfully. The receptionist and I had a friendly conversation, while I waited for my supervisor.

In a few minutes she appeared. I was invited into the conference room, where I found one of the other supervisors. That was a little unusual. She closed the door behind us and asked me to sit down. The room was eerily somber. After an awkward silence, she simply said," We're letting you go. We don't have a reason so you are free to collect unemployment."

Normally, in a situation like that, I would've been devastated. However, in this instance, I knew that God was at work. I was overcome with joy! It was all I could do to keep a smile from growing on my face. I wanted to laugh out loud. Instead, I calmly asked about my clients to make sure they would be provided for. Then I accepted their decision and walked out.

The moment I was outside of the office, I could not hold it in any longer. The joy in my heart exploded into jubilant laugher. I literally danced across the parking lot. I waited until after I climbed in the car, however, to shout, "Woooohooooo! Father, You are awesome!!!"

God absolutely amazed me that day! He prepared me first. Then, He accomplished it without me doing anything. I needed only to be willing and to give Him control.

God had restored me to my calling. Now I had time to write for Him.

CHAPTER 9
JEHOVAH JIREH, MY PROVIDER

"Therefore do not worry, saying,
'What shall we eat?' or 'What shall
we drink?' or 'What shall we wear?'
... For your heavenly Father knows
that you need all these things. But,
seek first the kingdom of God and
His righteousness, and all these things
shall be added to you." Matthew 6:31-33

Thoughts raced through my mind all the way home.

I had surrendered to God's will. He had prepared me emotionally.

I sought first the kingdom of God. My Father provided for my needs.

I allowed God to put His plan into action. He took care of everything, just as He promised He would.

I gave up the life that I had worked out for myself. He made sure I had time to devote to writing. I could finally pursue my calling.

When I arrived home, I sank to my knees in prayer. I was grateful for so many things.

"Lord," I prayed, "thank you for allowing me to witness Your awesome power in my life today. I am back in Your will now. I know You have the perfect plan for my life. Thank You for giving me time to pursue my calling; to write again. I pray that You continue to give me Your guidance. And place in my heart, the desire to seek it daily. I'm so grateful, Father, that You have provided for my necessities. You know what I need before I even ask. Thank You for loving me so much. I love You, too, Daddy!"

I sat silently then, soaking in His presence. Slowly, a memory came to my mind. Then suddenly, I realized that He had not only been preparing me in the last seven days, but much longer than that.

Two Years Earlier

I loved to shop at thrift stores. One day I was perusing the used books and came across Dave Ramsey's *Total Money Makeover*. I had heard Dave on the radio. I knew that he was a Christian and gave sound financial advice. I flipped through the book, then set it back down. I looked at more titles but kept coming back to that one. I finally gave in and bought it.

That evening I began reading. It grabbed my attention. I couldn't put it down. The concepts were so simple. They would take discipline but they made sense and were easy to understand. His system consisted of what he referred to as "Baby Steps."

I had been living paycheck to paycheck and had accumulated quite a bit of debt. My salary mostly went to making payments on each of the loans. If an emergency arose, like a flat tire or the washing machine broke down, I had to borrow from a credit card or go hungry. I really needed a money makeover!

The next day, I sat down with my finances and set up a plan. The first step was to establish a small emergency fund. I paid the minimum payment on my loans and set aside as much as I could every payday until I had saved $1,000. Yay! Step one was complete.

Step two was to pay off my debt. At that time, I had a car loan, medical bills, and several credit cards. Getting rid of those seemed overwhelming to me. However, the book had a solution for that. It was called the Debt Snowball.

I was skeptical at first. But, I planned it all out on paper and it worked. I could see myself succeeding.

Systematically, I paid extra on one of my loans (the same amount that I had been putting into my emergency fund). I started with the smallest one until that loan was paid off. Then, I used the amount I had been paying on that loan and put it toward the next smallest bill. One by one, my debts were paid in full.

Finally, the first two steps were complete. I had a small emergency fund; $1,000. All my debts (except my mortgage) were paid off. For the first time in years I was free of that burden. Yay! It felt so good.

My next step was to build a full emergency fund. That meant saving enough money to pay my bills for 3 to 6 months.

I had not spent money on anything but the essentials for the past year. I decided that I deserved to splurge a little. So, instead of saving all of the money I could, I started to indulge myself a little. After all, I felt pretty secure compared to where I was a year ago. And I was still saving some.

However, during my morning prayer times, I began feeling an urgency to save more money. I felt this message was from God, so I started listening. I cut my spending back to a minimum. I had just gotten a pay raise so I added that amount to my savings. All together, I was able to save around two-thousand dollars every month. I didn't know what God had in mind, but I trusted Him. Within nine months, my emergency account was more than fully funded. I had saved enough money to pay my bills for an entire year.

At that point, I wasn't aware of just how much I would need that money later on. But, God knew. He had been preparing me years ahead of time. I didn't know what was coming. I only trusted and obeyed. Now, I knew that nest egg was going to help me fulfill my calling.

I sought God first and, just as He promised, He provided the rest. Jehovah Jireh is truly my Provider.

CHAPTER 10
EXCEEDING MY DREAM TO WRITE

During the rest of those 40 days, I allowed God to guide me. He not only gave me time to write, but He inspired me to do something that I had only dreamed of before. I founded LIFE Ministries, a non-profit organization dedicated to discipling and encouraging Christians.

LIFE Ministries is an acronym for Living In the Father's Embrace. I love that title because it makes me picture a loving Father with His arms wrapped around me. It always makes me feel loved and secure.

I believe God gave me the name many years before. While going through some old files one day, I actually discovered some letterhead I had created about 20 years earlier. It was on purple paper and said, "Living In the Father's Embrace" across the top in fancy lettering. I didn't know anything about setting up a non-profit organization. However, with God's guidance, I was lead directly to the information that I needed. I sat down in a matter of a few hours and wrote out all of the details as He brought them to my mind. It just flowed. In the following days, I wrote up by-laws and a business plan. I knew this came from God, since I didn't have much experience in this area.

Since its inception, LIFE Ministries has become a website, www.livingintheFathersembrace.com, where I write encouraging articles about the Christian life. So far, I've produced some journals and coloring books that are available on Amazon. There is also a FaceBook Page and Pinterest account dedicated to the ministry. God only knows what else He will accomplish through this ministry.

One of my dreams has been to write books. I've been working on several different ones. However, God placed it on my heart to publish this book first. So, here it is: my debut book.

And all the glory goes to God!

CHAPTER 11
40 DAYS CAN CHANGE YOUR LIFE

"Be still and know that I am God."
Psalms 46:10

The experiences I had were unique. God has a different plan for each one of us. For instance, Jesus dealt with the rich, young ruler by asking him to sell all he had and give it to the poor. He didn't ask anyone else to do that. But, for the young ruler, his riches were coming between him and the Father.

You are one of a kind. Your relationship with our Father is unlike any other. When God creates your perfect plan, it is your very own. Take time to listen to Him. Let Him guide you on your own unique journey.

If you desire a closer relationship with our Father, I encourage you to take the 40-Day Challenge:

Commit a full 40 days

      to surrender yourself to God's will.

      Plan it out.

         Write it on your calendar.

Seek God diligently…

    First thing every morning.

      Start each day in quiet reflection.

Allow His Holy Spirit to flow into your soul.

    Breathe deeply.

      Soak Him in.

Know that He wants only the best for you.

        You can trust Him.

Then release your will.

      Let it go!

Ask your loving Father to open your eyes;

to show you anything that is

coming between you and Him.

Ask Him to reveal His will to you.

Then, quietly listen.

What does He bring to your mind?

A Bible verse?

Unconfessed sin?

Someone who needs help

or encouragement?

Be sure the message is truly from God.

Does is align with Scripture?

Is it in accord with

what you know of God's character?

Does it take you out of your comfort zone?

Will it benefit anyone but you?

When you are sure the message is from God:

Be willing to let go

of whatever is coming between you.

Be willing to follow His perfect plan for you.

Be willing to give Him control.

Let Him guide you…

step by step,

day by day.

See if He doesn't work powerfully in your life!

PRAYER OF SURRENDER

Here is a prayer that might be helpful to you on your 40-day journey:

Dear Father, Abba, Daddy,

I come to You, humbly asking that You show me Your will for my life. I know that You love me and want the very best for me. I trust You and surrender my will for Yours.

Show me if there is anything hindering our relationship, Lord. I will get rid of it! I don't want there to be anything between You and me.

Inspire me each day, Father. Let me understand Your will for me. Although You may not reveal Your entire plan at once, show me the next step.

Help me in any decisions I need to make. Guide me in making good choices, especially those that will affect others as well as myself.

Now I will be quiet before You, Father. I want to hear Your voice. Speak Your will to my heart and give me the strength I will need to be obedient.

I love You, Daddy!

A NOTE FROM THE AUTHOR

If you were blessed by this book or found it useful, I'd be grateful if you would post a short, honest review on Amazon. It's easy to do. Just go to this book's page on Amazon and click "Write A Customer Review."

Thank you so much for your support and feedback. It means so much! I personally read each review and will use this feedback to improve future books. God bless you!

BOOKS IN THIS SERIES

40 Days of Surrender: Journey to the Heart of God

40 Days of Surrender: Journey to the Heart of God
Large Print Version

40 Days of Surrender: Journey to the Heart of God
eBook Version

40 Days of Surrender Journal for Women

40 Days of Surrender Journal for Men

They can all be found on Amazon.

Just search: Karen Marshall Jennings

Thank you for your encouragement and support.

ABOUT THE AUTHOR

Karen Marshall Jennings felt called to write for God's glory in her early college days. Although many of her short stories and articles have been printed in Christian publications and newspaper throughout the years, she always had a passion for writing books. She just never had the time. That is until God worked a miracle in her life. Karen tells her amazing story in this, her debut book, 40 Days of Surrender, Journey to the Heart of God.

If you'd like to interact with Karen, you can find her in the 40 Days of Surrender Facebook group.

Karen is the founder of Living In the Father's Embrace Ministries. Find out more at LivingIntheFathersEmbrace.com and Living In the Father's Embrace Facebook or Pinterest page.

Karen attended Empire State College and received a degree in Counseling with a minor in Writing. She also has the gift of encouragement.

A PLACE FOR YOU TO
RECORD YOUR OWN JOURNEY

_____

_____

_____

_____

_____

_____

_____

_____

_____

_____

_____

_____

_____

_____

_____

_____

_____

_____

_____

_____

DATE_____

DATE_____

DATE_____

DATE_____

DATE_____

DATE_____

DATE_____

DATE_____

DATE_____

DATE_____

DATE_____

DATE_____

DATE_____

DATE_____

DATE_____

DATE_____

DATE_____

DATE_____

DATE_____

DATE_____

DATE_____

DATE_____

DATE_____

DATE_____

DATE_____

DATE_____

DATE_____

DATE_____

DATE_____

DATE_____

DATE_____

DATE_____

DATE_____

DATE_____

DATE_____

DATE_____

DATE_____

DATE_____

DATE_____

DATE_____

DATE_____

DATE_____

DATE_____

DATE_____

Made in the USA
Las Vegas, NV
03 March 2025

19008935R00059